Safe SOCIAL NETWORKING

By Barbara M. Linde

Gareth Stevens
Publishing

Please visit our website, www.garethstevens.com. For a free color catalog of all our high-quality books, call toll free 1-800-542-2595 or fax 1-877-542-2596.

Library of Congress Cataloging-in-Publication Data

Linde, Barbara M.
  Safe social networking / Barbara M. Linde.
      p. cm. — (Cyberspace survival guide)
  Includes index.
ISBN 978-1-4339-7229-4 (pbk.)
ISBN 978-1-4339-7230-0 (6-pack)
ISBN 978-1-4339-7228-7 (library binding)
1. Online social networks—Security measures. 2. Internet—Security measures. 3. Social networks. I. Title.
  HM742.L557 2013
  006.7'54—dc23
                                   2012012885

First Edition

Published in 2013 by
Gareth Stevens Publishing
111 East 14th Street, Suite 349
New York, NY 10003

Designer: Katelyn E. Reynolds
Editor: Therese M. Shea

Photo credits: Cover, p. 1 Thomas Tolstrup/Taxi/Getty Images; cover, pp. 1, 3–24 (background) Gala/Shutterstock.com; cover, pp. 1, 3–24 (grunge banner; cursor graphics; search box graphic) Amgun/Shutterstock.com; p. 4 Robbi/Shutterstock.com; p. 5 ©iStockphoto.com/Photomorphic; pp. 6, 28 iStockphoto/Thinkstock.com; p. 7 © iStockphoto.com/ardaguidogan; pp. 9, 19 (main image) Ron Chapple Studios/Thinkstock.com; p. 11 © iStockphoto.com/SamBurt; p. 13 Hasloo Group Production Studio/Shutterstock.com; p. 15 wawritto/Shutterstock.com; p. 17 Tony Avelar/ Bloomberg via Getty Images; p. 19 (screen image) Joe Corrigan/Getty Images for AOL; p. 21 © iStockphoto.com/abalcazar; p. 23 Hemera/Thinkstock.com; p. 24 Lisa F. Young/Shutterstock.com; p. 27 Richard Hutchings/Photo Researchers/Getty Images.

Printed in the United States of America

CPSIA compliance information: Batch #CS12GS: For further information contact Gareth Stevens, New York, New York at 1-800-542-2595.

CONTENTS

🔍 Words in the glossary appear in **bold** type the first time they are used in the text.

What Is a SOCIAL NETWORK?

Do you have family members? Do you have friends? What about teachers, neighbors, or other community members? Of course you do! They're all parts of your social network.

A social network is a group of people who know each other. You can belong to several social networks at the same time. Your family social network might include parents, brothers, sisters, grandparents, cousins, aunts, and uncles. Your principal, teachers, cooks, bus drivers, and students are all members of your school social network. Your friends make up another social network. You're all connected, like a kind of web.

Social Network

4

🔍 What Does Your Social Network Look Like?

Make a social-network web. Draw a circle in the middle of a piece of paper and put your name in it. Now write the names of each of your friends in surrounding circles. Draw a line from your name to each friend's name. If your friends also know each other, draw lines to connect their names. How does your network look?

The members of your social network probably talk to each other and do things together. Having a social network helps people feel happy and safe.

5

What Is a Social NETWORKING SITE?

An online social network is a group of people who use the Internet to communicate with each other. A social networking site is a website that makes it easy for its group members to connect online. It allows people to share messages, chat, and see photos and videos. Facebook, Myspace, Tagged, Twitter, and Google+ are all kinds of social networking sites.

You can use any kind of computer that connects to the Internet to join a social networking site. You can connect through a desktop or laptop computer. Perhaps you have a small electronic tablet, smartphone, or other handheld device to carry everywhere. You can connect through that, too.

🔍 Are You Old Enough?

Many social networking sites won't let you register if you're under a certain age. For Facebook, 13 is the magic number. Myspace requires you to be 14 or older. Each website has a "Terms" page, so have your parents help you check out the requirements.

Welcome to Facebook
//www.facebook.com/

facebook

Twitter

 http

Linked in ®

Home   What is LinkedIn?   Jo

Over 120 mil

exchange in

 http://twitter.com/

twitter 🐦

 https://plus.google.com

Google+: real life sharing, rethought for th

+You   Gmail   Calendar   Documents   Photos   Sites   Web   More ▾

Follow

Instant updates

celebrities, and

Google+

 www.blogg

Google

YouTube – Broadcast Yourself.

 http://www.youtube.com/

B Blogger

Create a blog. It's free

The Internet has made it easy to share our thoughts with others. We just need to make sure that we're sharing with the right people.

nnity!

7

Lorem Ipsum

Already have an account? Sign In

Account?

When you were younger, you wouldn't cross the street without help from your parents. You shouldn't start out on the Internet's **information** superhighway without them either! It's important to let your parents know what you're doing online. They can help you find social networking sites that are right for you.

You can't possibly know everyone who may see your information online. It can actually be dangerous to talk to older kids or to adults you don't know. Parents can help spot suspicious activity and take action if necessary. They can help keep the Internet fun for you and your friends.

🔍 Back in the Old Days

E-mail didn't even exist before 1971. When it was first invented, it was only used by people sharing a single computer. Later, e-mail was used in a small network. The first web **browser** was invented in 1990. After that, new networks were created, and more people could connect.

You may be able to teach your parents about Internet safety and social networking by sharing computer time with them.

Using Privacy SETTINGS

Each social networking site has privacy settings. Always read the website's information about them. Set yours at the highest level of security. That means your information cannot be viewed by just anyone. You decide who your friends are, and you decide which of those friends can see some or all of your information.

Why are privacy settings so important? Online posts are never completely private. Without privacy controls, your information might go to hundreds or thousands of people. Strangers can comment on your posts and share your information with others. People you don't even know can find out all about you.

🔍 Tag—You're It!

Tagging is labeling someone in a photo. Your privacy settings should let you know when you're tagged in a photo. You can reject the tagging if you don't want to be linked to the photo. You can also ask the person to remove the photo from their post.

10

Choose your privacy settings

 Connecting on Facebook

Control basic information your friends will use

Facebook

11

Those settings control who can see wh

Acceptable Use POLICIES

An acceptable use **policy**, or AUP, is a set of rules for a website. It's available on the site and may be labeled "Terms of Service." Before using a site, you usually have to read the policy and click in a box to show that you accept the terms. If you don't accept the AUP, you can't fully access the website. If you do accept the terms and then disobey them, you might have your account removed.

An AUP helps people know what behavior to expect of other people on the social networking site. AUPs usually warn people about posting inappropriate photos and using bad language.

🔍 What's Your AUP?

If your school has a website or has computers in classrooms, it probably has an acceptable use policy. You and your parents might have signed an AUP so you can use the school's computers and its network. That means you and other students are responsible for your online actions. Check your school handbook.

Many people accept the AUP without reading it well. Be smart and know what you're getting into before you click "I agree."

Screen Names and PASSWORDS

When you log on to a social networking site, you need to create a screen name, or username. This is the name that is connected to your messages and to your account. Don't ever use your real name, age, street address, or e-mail address as part of your screen name. Here's an unwise screen name: *MargieGreene9EvansvilleIllinois*. This screen name is much better: *MRainbowG*.

Your password is like a key that unlocks the door to the website. It should be a combination of letters, numbers, and characters. It shouldn't be easy to figure out. Which of these passwords do you think is best: *FrankLee* or *Fr8nkL*? The second one, of course!

🔍 What's in a Name?

Many sites allow only one person to have a screen name, so you may have to try several names before you get one you can use. There are websites to help you find or create good screen names and passwords, but it can be a lot of fun thinking of your own. And you'll probably remember them better.

14

Username: Login

Password: ●●●●●

Submit

Keep your username and password a secret from everyone but your parents. If you have to write them down to remember them, put the paper in a safe place.

15

Your PROFILE

To create your **profile**, you'll fill in a form on the website. Be careful when you do this. Think of the people who will see the profile. Unless you know the website is **secure**, don't post a picture of yourself. Don't include the name of your school. You don't want strangers to find or contact you.

You can still give information about your interests without getting too personal. After all, would you tell someone *everything* about yourself when you first meet? Probably not. Just include a few things, such as your taste in music and books. That's enough to find friends of similar interests.

🔍 Your Personal Statement

Some sites let you write a personal statement. Read this personal statement: *I love water sports like swimming and snorkeling. My favorite singers are Taylor Swift and Selena Gomez. True Jackson is a cool show. Call me a nerd, but I love science class!* You can tell a lot about this person without knowing too much personal information.

You can change your social networking site profile from laptops, desktops, and handheld computers.

Online Etiquette? YOU BET!

Are you polite to adults and other kids that you see? Of course you are! You should observe the same **etiquette** online. All you see is the computer screen, but there's a person at the other end of that cyberspace connection. So remember your manners! Here are some quick and easy ways to type polite words:

```
please              = pls
thank you very much = tyvm
keep in touch       = kit
best friend         = bf
good to see you     = g2cu
I am sorry          = ims
```

Also, DON'T SHOUT in capital letters too much. No one enjoys being yelled at. Use regular **fonts** and proper punctuation.

Check the address box to make sure you're sending a message to the right person! People sometimes click on Reply All instead of Reply when responding to an e-mail. If you put a paper letter in your mailbox by accident, you can run out and get it before the mail carrier comes. But once you click on the Send button, that's it.

twitter

@jenny123 G2cu. Let's play again tomorrow. How about 7 PM? kit

↩ Reply ⇄ Retweet

42 minutes ago via web

amym
Amy

About Us   Contact   Blog   Status   Goodies   API   Business   Help   Jobs   Terms   Policy

© 2011 Twitter

You and your friends can have fun making up your own polite shortcut words!

Save

Email

Text

Tumblr

YouTube

Facebook

Twitter

3G

08:10

13:47

12:35

12:26

12:23

12:15

12:04

11:46

Before you comment, consider if you would
like to read the same thing about yourself.

20

You can change or rip up something you write on paper. You can't do that when you post something on a social networking site. Sure, you can delete it. But even if you do, someone may have copied it and saved it on their computer, and you may never know.

Let's say you post a mean or rude comment about another person. Years later, you apply for a job. The employers might look you up on the Internet and find your rude comment. They'll wonder if you would be a good employee. This really happens to people, so think before you write.

🔍 Guard Your Privacy!

Don't give out your address, phone number, or names of family members. Don't tell anyone you chat with online what you look like. If you're wondering whether or not to write something, imagine that your text is written in the newspaper for the whole world to see. If that thought makes you uncomfortable, don't write it.

When Problems POP UP

Sometimes, even if you're being safe and respectful, you can find trouble on social networking sites. "Trolls" are people who post hurtful attacks on message boards or other group sites. They may also change the subject of a discussion to whatever they want to talk about.

In online multiplayer games, "griefers" are people who try to ruin your fun. They may place **obstacles** in your path, send nasty messages, or kill your character in an unsportsmanlike way.

Social Networks Go to School

Social networking may seem like all fun, but it can be used for learning, too. Some schools encourage the use of social networking. Imagine having an online chat with your principal or a teacher. Students may do **research** together. They can publish their work online and get quick feedback.

You can never know why trolls and griefers act the way they do. It's best just to stay away if possible. You can report them to website operators, too.

Do yourself and your friends a favor and don't put up with cyberbullies. There are ways to get them off websites.

Cyberbullies are another problem on social networking sites. A cyberbully might insult you, threaten you, or give out your private information. Some cyberbullies steal your password and pretend to be you online. Do you know what to do if you meet up with cyberbullies? Tell your parents, teachers, or other helpful adults. They can contact the website operators for help.

Many AUPs address cyberbullying because it has become a major issue for young people today. No one needs to live with bullying. It's actually brave to report cyberbullies. You'll be helping yourself and other kids fight against them.

🔍 Zip Your Lips!

Don't ever answer an attack by a cyberbully. Sometimes it's hard not to, but you'll only make matters worse. You could even be accused of cyberbullying yourself if your message seems angry or mean. It often doesn't matter who "started it." You might lose your account on the site.

Kids-Only SAFE SITES

Are you too young for Facebook or some other social networking sites? No problem! Log on to kids-only interactive sites. These sites are **designed** for people ages 6 to 14, but parents must still help kids sign up. Most sites ask for a parent or guardian's e-mail address or other contact information.

Once you're signed up, you can create a profile. Some sites require a photo so the website's operators can make sure you're really you when you sign on. The content **filters** keep out bad language, bullies, and strangers. Kids like you can enjoy safe social networking.

🔍 Social Networking 4 Kids!

What's What?
www.whatswhat.me
- play games
- make profile pages
- post photos and videos
- **friend** people the same age

giantHello
www.gianthello.com
- friending
- play games
- instant messaging
- chat on fan pages

Franktown Rocks!
www.franktownrocks.com
- play multiplayer game
- create characters
- make and listen to music
- watch videos

Several computer programs protect kids from unsafe websites. If you try to go to a **restricted** site, you'll be blocked. Your parents may get notified, too!

Be Social—STAY SAFE!

Being part of an online social network can be fun. You're able to keep in touch with family and friends, both near and far away. You can meet all kinds of people from all over the world.

But remember that the people in your online social network are just that—people. They have feelings and opinions. They should be treated with respect, just like you treat the people around you every day. Also remember that just as you need to be careful around strangers, you need to be watchful of online strangers. Now log on and start social networking!

privacy settings

appropriate shared information

Q **Safe Social Networking**

parental controls

secure sites

proper etiquette

GLOSSARY

browser: a computer program that allows a user to get onto the Internet and look at information

design: to create the pattern or structure of something

etiquette: the rules governing correct or polite behavior

filter: a tool that allows some items to pass and blocks others

font: a set of screen characters of the same style and size

friend: to add someone as a friend on a social networking site

information: knowledge or facts

obstacle: something that blocks a path

policy: a course or method of action to guide decisions

profile: a collection of facts about someone, especially on a website

research: the collecting of information to learn more about a topic

restrict: to keep something within limits

secure: safe and protected from harm by others

For More INFORMATION

Books

Jakubiak, David J. *A Smart Kid's Guide to Social Networking Online.* New York, NY: PowerKids Press, 2010.

Lüsted, Marcia Amidon. *Social Networking: MySpace, Facebook, & Twitter.* Edina, MN: ABDO Publishing, 2011.

Ryan, Peter K. *Social Networking.* New York, NY: Rosen Central, 2010.

Websites

Social Networking Sites: Safety Tips for Tweens and Teens
www.ftc.gov/bcp/edu/pubs/consumer/tech/tec14.shtm
Follow this advice from the Federal Trade Commission when you join a social networking site.

Ten Safe Social Networking Sites for Kids
www.npr.org/2011/07/11/137705552/ten-safe-social-networking-sites-for-kids
Check out this list of social networking sites just for your age group.

INDEX